SO-ALI-518

ULTIMATE TEDDY
B·E·A·R

THE LITTLE BOOK OF
BEAR CARE

PAULINE COCKRILL

Introduction by Judy Sparrow

Reader's Digest

The Reader's Digest Association (Canada) Ltd.
Montreal

A DORLING KINDERSLEY BOOK

PROJECT EDITOR Polly Boyd   ART EDITOR Vicki James
MANAGING EDITOR Mary-Clare Jerram   MANAGING ART EDITOR Gill Della Casa
PRODUCTION MANAGER Eunice Paterson

PUBLISHED IN CANADA IN 1992
BY THE READER'S DIGEST ASSOCIATION (CANADA) LTD.
215 REDFERN AVENUE, WESTMOUNT, QUEBEC H3Z 2V9

FIRST PUBLISHED IN GREAT BRITAIN IN 1992
BY DORLING KINDERSLEY LIMITED,
9 HENRIETTA STREET, LONDON WC2E 8PS
COPYRIGHT © 1992 DORLING KINDERSLEY LIMITED, LONDON

Canadian Cataloguing in Publication Data
Cockrill, Pauline
    The little bear library

Contents: [v. 1] The little book of bear care.– [v. 2] The little book of celebrity bears. –
    [v. 3] The little book of traditional bears.
Each title also issued separately.
ISBN 0–88850–199–4 (set) – ISBN 0–88850–197–8 (v. 1) –
ISBN 0–88850–196–X (v. 2) – ISBN 0–88850–195–1 (v. 3)

1. Teddy bears – History. 2. Teddy bears – History – Pictorial works. 3. Teddy bears –
Repairing. 4. Teddy bears – Collectors and collecting. 5. Teddy bears – Pictorial works.
I. Title. II. Title: The little book of bear care. III. Title: The little book of celebrity bears.
IV. Title: The little book of traditional bears.
NK8740.C63 1992   688.7'24   C92–090298–7

Computer page make-up by The Cooling Brown Partnership, Great Britain
Text film output by The Right Type, Great Britain
Reproduced by Colourscan, Singapore
Printed in Hong Kong

92 93 94 95 96 / 5 4 3 2 1

⚮·Contents·⚮

Introduction 4

Eyes
Repairing Traditional Bears 6
Repairing Modern Bears 8

Nose & Mouth
Repairing Traditional and
Modern Bears 10

Body Fabrics
Repairing Traditional Bears 12
Repairing Modern Bears 14

Paw & Footpads
Repairing Traditional Bears 16
Repairing Modern Bears 18

Joints
Repairing Traditional and
Modern Bears 20

Sound Boxes
Repairing Traditional Bears 22
Repairing Modern Bears 24

Seams
Repairing Traditional and
Modern Bears 26

Stuffings
Repairing Traditional and
Modern Bears 28

Washing
Caring for Traditional and
Modern Bears 30

Grooming
Caring for Traditional and
Modern Bears 32

Bear Wear
Accessories for Traditional and
Modern Bears 34

Storage
Caring for Traditional and
Modern Bears 36

Bear Owners 38
Useful Addresses 39
Index 40
Acknowledgments 41

❧ INTRODUCTION ·❧

by Judy Sparrow

For those who inherit or buy a valuable antique bear, or perhaps have just discovered their long-lost childhood toy in the attic, one of the most important considerations is the bear's condition and future care. The love that is given to all bears by their owners means a hard life for a teddy. Many are slept on, squashed, and cried over – even torn apart by jealous siblings or attacked by dogs. The box in the dusty attic where a teddy has spent many years waiting to see again the light of day may also be home to insects, and the back of the garage is probably damp.

———— ·❧·❧· ————

Almost any bear can be restored to a sound and strong condition, but a badly worn teddy does need expert attention. The straightforward repairs in this book are easy

A COLLECTOR'S BEAR
Protect a valuable antique bear with clothing, like this sumptuous blue velvet jacket and breeches.

4

enough for anybody who can sew a seam. The basic rules are: always use very strong thread; start and finish seams thoroughly; examine seams for broken stitches and resew immediately; never cut off tattered ends of paws or feet, or loose legs, arms, or ears; never use glue on the body of a fabric bear.

PATIENT BEAR
A 1950s bear waits for his operation.

Although collectible and antique bears should be restored to as close to the original condition as possible, many children's toys have immense sentimental value: the pads are scraps of mother's old skirt, or the eyes are buttons from grandma's sewing box. Changing everything on a family bear may not be necessary. However, loose limbs, and the consequent strain on a threadbare stomach from the joints, or the rusty wire of a broken squeaker, may be more dangerous to a teddy's long-term health.

Bears benefit from the right clothes – a knitted suit will protect and enhance a threadbare teddy. In the same way, correct period clothing makes it safer to handle an antique bear. Even the bear sitting at the foot of a child's bed is more likely to survive for the next generation if he is clothed and cared for from the first day he is welcomed into the family.

A FAMILY BEAR
This 1950s Chad Valley bear is basically in good condition. A washing and brushing, and a ribbon bow, are all that is needed to restore his appearance.

❧·EYES·❧
Repairing Traditional Bears

Trouser buttons are an unusual replacement for the original glass eyes.

Original mohair plush fabric, now almost worn away in places.

Alpha Toys trademark label, sewn on foot-pad.

Replacement felt paws and footpads.

1930s FARNELL BEAR

he earliest teddies had black or – occasionally – brown boot-button eyes. Blown glass eyes generally replaced these in the 1920s as buttoned boots (and their buttons) left the fashion scene. Modern replicas of both types are available but should be used only on bears that are not intended for use as children's toys.

▷ **ORIGINAL WOODEN BOOT BUTTONS** have a small, rounded metal shank on the back. Black is the most usual color for the eyes of traditional bears.

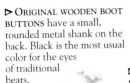

▷ **POLYESTER THREAD** secures the eyes through the shank.

▷ **PLASTIC BUTTONS** can replace boot buttons.

△ **CLEAR GLUE** dabbed in eye socket gives a secure repair.

◁ **CLEAR GLASS EYES** were often backed with brown enamel.

△ **ARTISTS' ACRYLIC PAINT** can be useful for coloring clear glass eyes.

▷ **WIRED GLASS EYES** are joined in pairs. Snip apart to make two short wire stems. Twist the wire with pliers to form a shank.

▽ **MERCERIZED COTTON** makes safe embroidered eyes for a child's bear.

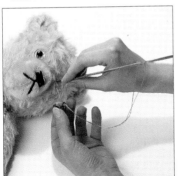

◁ **SHANKED EYES** are attached by bringing strong thread through the head, into the eye socket, and through the shank. Return thread to back of head and secure with several stitches.

❧ Eyes ❧

Repairing Modern Bears

A bandage used as a first-aid remedy for a lost eye may damage the fabric.

Yellow-and-black plastic safety eye is locked securely in position with a toothed washer.

This modern bear is made of good quality synthetic plush.

CONTEMPORARY PLUSH BEAR

By the 1950s, molded glass and plastic eyes had become the most widely used varieties. The wire shank evolved into an integral plastic shank with a separate washer. This created the safety eye that is now required for all children's toys. Replica boot buttons and glass eyes are still commonly used for collectors' bears, to achieve a traditional appearance.

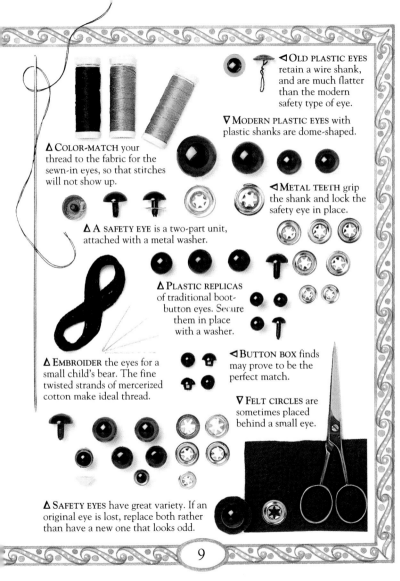

◁ OLD PLASTIC EYES retain a wire shank, and are much flatter than the modern safety type of eye.

▽ MODERN PLASTIC EYES with plastic shanks are dome-shaped.

△ COLOR-MATCH your thread to the fabric for the sewn-in eyes, so that stitches will not show up.

◁ METAL TEETH grip the shank and lock the safety eye in place.

△ A SAFETY EYE is a two-part unit, attached with a metal washer.

△ PLASTIC REPLICAS of traditional boot-button eyes. Secure them in place with a washer.

△ EMBROIDER the eyes for a small child's bear. The fine twisted strands of mercerized cotton make ideal thread.

◁ BUTTON BOX finds may prove to be the perfect match.

▽ FELT CIRCLES are sometimes placed behind a small eye.

△ SAFETY EYES have great variety. If an original eye is lost, replace both rather than have a new one that looks odd.

❧·NOSE & MOUTH·❧
Repairing Traditional and Modern Bears

A leather patch replaces nose and the surrounding worn fabric.

The missing mouth gives an endearing doleful expression.

The original black leather paw pads match those on the feet.

Typical 1940s bear made of real sheepskin dyed golden brown.

1940s SHEEPSKIN BEAR

A hand-stitched nose and mouth are classic features of both traditional and modern bears. While the nose is sometimes made of molded rubber or plastic, or even painted tin, the mouth is invariably stitched in the traditional inverted Y-shape so often associated with bears: a central, vertical stitch with a single or double horizontal stitch.

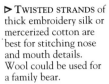

▷ TWISTED STRANDS of thick embroidery silk or mercerized cotton are best for stitching nose and mouth details. Wool could be used for a family bear.

△ STITCHED NOSES AND MOUTHS are commonly black or brown. The vertical stitch catches a horizontal stitch to form the typical inverted Y-shaped mouth.

△ NEEDLES with large eyes are best.

△ TIN NOSES are more suitable for old bears. They are sewn on-to the muzzle through holes at the sides of the nostrils.

△ STRONG THREAD must be used to attach sewn-on noses, but do not use such noses on a child's toy.

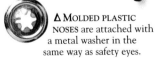

△ MOLDED PLASTIC NOSES are attached with a metal washer in the same way as safety eyes.

◁ THIN, FINE LEATHER or stretchy cotton fabric are less usual, but possible, choices for the nose of a family bear.

11

❧ Body Fabrics ·❧
Repairing Traditional Bears

1910 Steiff bear made of black mohair plush.

Fabric often tears near joints.

Torn fabric weakens the whole arm.

Replacement beige suede footpads.

1910 STEIFF BEAR

The early teddy bear manufacturers abandoned the expensive real fur that had always been used for other toy animals, in favor of a newly invented and cheaper material called mohair plush. Woven from a combination of long, silky Angora-goat hair and cotton or wool, this luxurious fabric is regarded as the hallmark of a quality bear.

▷ WOVEN MOHAIR PLUSH comes in a wide range of traditional colors. Using any other material to patch an old mohair bear will devalue the bear, but a new piece must have the same length of pile and weave as the original fabric.

△ COTTON OR POLYESTER THREAD can be used to sew seams and patches.

△ MOHAIR PLUSH straight from the loom has long and shaggy separate strands. Clipping and brushing create a short, dense pile.

△ DISTRESSED MOHAIR – a 1980s' invention – is treated to look like the fabric of very old bears.

△ MULTIPURPOSE DYES can darken a patching piece that has the right weave and pile, but is the wrong shade. Mix colors to get a match.

△ THE REVERSE SIDE OF WOVEN MOHAIR can be used to patch a bald bear. The weave should match that of the bear's original fabric to achieve the most authentic look.

△ OLD PIECES OF FABRIC are useful for patching a bear whose mohair has lost some of its pile.

△ A NATURAL-FIBER BRISTLE BRUSH will fluff up the pile of a much-cuddled bear.

⋅❧ BODY FABRICS ❧⋅
Repairing Modern Bears

Worn fabric around nose and mouth.

Details must be stitched again after repair has been made.

Bear made of natural undyed sheepskin.

Most of the fabric is still in good condition.

Bears of this period were often stuffed with cotton waste.

Sheepskin becomes brittle and tears easily.

LATE 1940S SHEEPSKIN BEAR

The 1940s saw the beginning of an increased popularity in materials made from synthetic fibers. Acrylic, nylon, and artificial silk plush – the most widely used fabrics – are produced on a knitted or woven backing. They make surface-washable bears that are especially suitable for children. Real mohair plush is still favored for collectors' bears.

▷ **WOVEN SHORT-PILE** and **DISTRESSED MOHAIR PLUSH** are expensive fabrics. A modern bear's fur is probably not worn, but torn, so you may need only a small piece, such as a remnant, for patching.

▽ **COTTON PLUSH** is a natural fabric with a woven backing. It is much less expensive than real mohair.

◁ **REAL SHEEPSKIN** can be difficult to work with.
▽ **SYNTHETIC SHEEPSKIN** makes a good alternative.

◁ **THREADS** for hand-stitching are stronger if used double.

△ **REPAIRING SHEEPSKIN** is not easy, as the skin dries out with age and often becomes too brittle to sew. A piece of supple kid leather makes an excellent repair – an old glove could provide a big enough patch. Cut a piece that is slightly larger than the area to be repaired, and glue it to the inside with rubber cement.

▷ **SYNTHETIC FABRICS** come in an enormous range of colors and finishes. A patch must match the length of pile as well as the color of material used originally. You can clip shaggy, long-haired types to get the right length.

❧ · PAW & FOOTPADS · ❧
Repairing Traditional Bears

1950s bear made of golden mohair plush.

Fabric and stuffing may need total replacement.

Worn paw pad shows old cotton waste stuffing.

Original, threadbare Rexine footpad.

Seams are often the first area to come apart.

1950S GOLDEN MOHAIR PLUSH BEAR

Felt was the most common material for the paw and foot-pads of traditional bears; it is still first choice for patching and replacing those worn beyond repair. Rexine, a treated muslin that is no longer available, was used from the 1930s to about 1960. Tightly woven cotton fabric, painted with artists' quick-drying acrylic, makes an effective substitute.

▷ **COTTON THREAD** is best for machined seams.

◁ **HAT FELT** is used to replace dense felt pads.

▽ **CARDBOARD** reinforces the footpads of standing bears.

▷ **NEEDLES** for hand-stitching must be sharp.

△ **POLYESTER** makes strong thread.

△ **FLANNELETTE** was used on bears made in the 1930s.

▽ **FAKE REXINE** has a closely woven cotton base material.

△ **FELT PATCHES** must match the original fabric. Ladder-stitch neatly in place (see p.27) using polyester thread.

▽ **ACRYLIC PAINT** is applied to the fabric with a soft brush.

△ **EMBROIDERED CLAWS** in mercerized cotton add a final touch of detailing.

❧ PAW & FOOTPADS ❧
Repairing Modern Bears

Golden mohair plush fabric is mostly in reasonable condition.

Safe plastic eyes locked into place with a washer.

Pedigree Soft Toys bear, made in the Belfast factory around 1955.

Velveteen paw and footpads have lost much of the surface pile, but seams are still intact.

1950S MOHAIR BEAR

ince the 1950s, a whole array of materials has joined the felt that was once used almost exclusively for bear pads. Modern-day manufacturers now have to choose from natural fabrics, such as woven cottons, velveteen, colored felts, leather, and suede, and synthetic nylon plush, suedette, and leatherette.

▷ **POLYESTER** and **COTTON THREAD** are equally suitable for hand-sewing patches.

▽ **CARDBOARD** or iron-on interlining can strengthen thinner fabrics.

▷ **SYNTHETIC VELVET** has a close texture, almost no pile, and very little stretch.

▷ **SUEDETTE**, a synthetic material, looks quite different from suede.

▷ **COTTON VELVETEEN** has a close-woven backing and a short, thick pile.

△ **FELT** is ideal for patching and replacing pads as the edges do not fray. Thick types are hard-wearing.

◁ **LEATHERETTE** has some give, making it easier to work with than real leather.

◁ **KNITTED** fabric stretches and will fit neatly over worn pads.

△ **SUEDE** is expensive, but a patching piece can be cut from a new pair of cheap slippers.

◁ **WOVEN MOHAIR PLUSH** is sometimes reversed for pads.

◁ **CLIPPED NYLON PLUSH** is commonly used for pads.

▷ **THREAD** for the claws must match the color of nose and mouth.

❖ JOINTS ❖
Repairing Traditional and Modern Bears

1950s English bear made of mohair plush, colored golden when new.

New boot-button eyes.

Badly worn arm joint needs to be replaced.

Original flannelette paw pads.

Original flannelette footpads.

1950S MOHAIR BEAR

Most traditional bears – and traditional-style modern ones – have a movable head and limbs. Their joints work on the enduring principle of two disks rotating around a pin; it is only the disk and pin materials, and the fixing method, that have changed over the years. The modern washable teddy bears are usually unjointed.

△ **TO REPAIR** a traditional Masonite joint, you need two disks, two washers, and one cotter pin. Open the main body seam (see p.27). Place a disk and washer on a pin in the top of the limb, and close the seam. Push the pin into the body, slide on the disk and washer, and bend the pin ends, with pliers, close to the disk. Sew up the main seam.

▽ **CARDBOARD** was the material from which joints were originally made. The two disks are held together by a short metal pin inserted through a central hole, reinforced with metal washers.

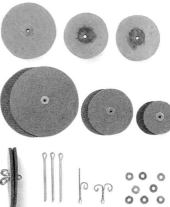

△ **MASONITE** does not disintegrate as quickly as cardboard and so makes stronger, longer-lasting disks. Use it to cut your own disks, together with new metal washers and cotter pins.

▷ **A SPECIAL TOOL** for fixing plastic disks is available.

△ **MODERN JOINTS** are made entirely of plastic, in a variety of sizes. Each disk has an integral molded pin with grooves that allow the washer to be pushed along the pin but ensure that it cannot move once fixed in position.

◁ **PLASTIC DISKS** with molded pins and metal washers are fixed in the same way as modern safety eyes (see p.9). They form very secure joints.

❧ SOUND BOXES ❧
Repairing Traditional Bears

Early Steiff bear made of long, shaggy black mohair plush.

Worn-out voice box can be felt inside body, but the bear produces no sound.

Main seam is at front, not back, of body.

Original wood-wool stuffing.

EARLY STEIFF BEAR

Mechanisms to give teddies a voice have been used since the early days. Punch and tilt growlers and squeakers contain a reed that produces a sound as air is forced over it. Music boxes have worked by a clockwork movement since the 1930s; prior to this the cylinder was turned by a system of springs and levers, operated by squeezing.

▷ **EARLY TILT GROWLER** has a lead weight that opens and closes hinged bellows as the bear is tilted from back to front. The action makes a reed, attached inside a cardboard tube, vibrate.

▽ **SQUEAKERS** were used before growlers. They, too, contain a reed that creates the sound. The recoil of the spring inside produces the necessary rush of air as the bear is squeezed.

△ **THIS 1930S TILT GROWLER** has a porcelain weight with a reed set into it, and sliding oilcloth bellows. Air and sound escape through a waxed-paper membrane. The other growler shown above is contained in a cardboard container with a perforated lid that allows the sound through.

▽ **A MUSIC BOX** contains a clockwork-driven cylinder with pins on the surface and a metal plate divided into teeth of varying lengths. As the cylinder turns, the pins strike the teeth to produce different notes, creating a tune.

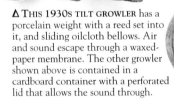

◁ **WOOD WOOL** around a new voice box allows air to be sucked in, but cannot clog the mechanism. An old box may be past repair, except by a specialist (see p.39).

23

❧ SOUND BOXES ❧

Repairing Modern Bears

1980s bear made of golden nylon plush.

Dark brown velveteen paw and footpads.

Bear has been slept on, flattening the tummy fabric and squashing the squeaker.

1980S NYLON PLUSH BEAR

Modern voice-making devices are essentially the same as those used in older bears. Growlers still contain a weight, bellows, and reed, now enclosed in a plastic case. Squeakers – invariably made of thin plastic – still contain a reed, but are now enclosed in a plastic tube. Music boxes are wound using a pull cord or key.

◁ **GROWLER MECHANISMS** have been housed inside molded plastic canisters since the 1940s. The whole unit may lack the aesthetic appeal of earlier models, but it does the job just as efficiently and withstands a considerable amount of rough handling.

▽ **PLASTIC SQUEAKERS** come in various forms; they may be flat, concertina, or barrel-shaped with a spring. The squeak is produced by the vibration of a metal and plastic reed, protected by a hollow plastic tube.

◁ **BELLS** in the ears were first used in 1957 by the British company Merrythought. Although other bear manufacturers copied this idea, bells have never been as popular as squeakers and growlers.

▽ **POLYESTER** is the best stuffing to pack around a modern bear's voice box. The fine fibers in kapok (see p.29) make it an unsuitable material for the job.

▷ **PLASTIC CASES** enclose many modern music boxes. The clockwork movement here is probably Japanese and can be activated by a nylon pull cord.

◁ **MUSIC BOXES** work on the original principle: metal teeth of different lengths strike against pins on a revolving cylinder, sounding different notes to create a tune.

❧·SEAMS·❧

Repairing Traditional and Modern Bears

Original long mohair plush is very worn and dirty.

Machine-sewn front seam shows that main hand-stitched body seam is at back of bear.

Emergency bandage holds together a split seam.

Dirty pink velveteen pads can be surface-washed or replaced.

Wood-wool stuffing.

1930S MOHAIR BEAR

Whether old or new, a bear is made from pieces of fabric, most of which are sewn together by machine. The main body seam is the important exception. It is always stitched by hand. Bears are often flung around and carried by their limbs, so the arm and leg seams are the ones that are most likely to come apart.

▽ **LADDER STITCH** is recommended for externally sewn seams. Fold under the raw edges. Bring up the thread from inside, cross to the other side, and take a stitch behind, along the channel, coming out just above.

◁ **THREAD** for sewing seams by hand should be of heavier weight than all-purpose cottons. The type sold for top-stitching is ideal, or use ordinary thread doubled.

△ **POLYESTER THREAD** withstands strain a little better than cotton. Whichever you use, choose a color that blends with the fabric.

△ **PULL UP THE THREAD** after every two or three stitches to bring the sides of the seam together. The tiny stitches on the outside of the join will be barely visible. Finish off firmly at the end of the seam. Use this stitch for patching.

△ **THE MAIN SEAM** running the length of the bear's body is the only point of access for major body repairs, such as renewing joints (see p.21) or replacing the sound box (see pp.23 & 25). It is usually at the back, but is at the front on early Steiff bears. The last seam to be completed, it is stitched by hand.

❧ STUFFINGS ❧

Repairing Traditional and Modern Bears

Joints rub against stuffing, causing it and the fabric to wear thin.

Stuffing is often lost first around top of arms.

British bear in need of complete overhaul.

Original wood-wool stuffing.

EARLY 1930S MOHAIR BEAR

he material with which a bear is stuffed rapidly transforms a few pieces of fabric into a cuddly friend. The early manufacturers used wood wool, and then kapok. Later, shredded plastic foam – popular from the 1950s – ensured a fully washable bear. Nowadays, polyester wadding satisfies even the most stringent modern safety standards.

▷ **WOOD WOOL,** also known as excelsior, is made from long, fine wood shavings, chopped into shorter strands. Old fairground toys often contain wood wool and may yield enough for a small repair.

◁ **SILKY KAPOK** attracts neither insects nor rodents and is a good choice for a natural fiber stuffing. Do not use it for packing around a squeaker or growler; fine fibers will clog the mechanism.

▷ **SHREDDED PLASTIC FOAM** has some advantage over natural materials. Bears stuffed with it can be immersed in water for washing – but remember that burning foam emits toxic fumes.

◁ **POLYESTER WADDING** stuffs many modern bears, particularly unjointed types. It is a cheap, hygienic, safe filling for a family bear, and is ideal for packing sound boxes (see p.25).

▷ **ACRYLIC WASTE** is the modern synthetic version of the various stuffings that once utilized the waste materials of cotton and woolen mills. It is important, when replacing a bear's stuffing, to try to use the same type as the original, so even this material has its place.

❧ WASHING ❧

Caring for Traditional and Modern Bears

New amber and black glass eyes.

Nose and mouth have been restitched to match claws.

Mohair plush is quite dirty where pile has been lost.

Worn foot-pads have been repaired before washing bear.

1930s CHAD VALLEY BEAR

A clean bear not only looks its best, but also has a longer life than its grubby, neglected cousin. The body fabric of most teddies can at least be surface-washed, although felt, velveteen, and cotton plush cannot. Check for insect damage (see p.37) and mend any damaged parts before starting to spruce up your bear.

▷ A BABY'S BRUSH and
COMB are gentle enough to
use on old and fragile
fabrics.

▽ TERRY TOWELS quickly absorb
any excess moisture. Use white
towels to keep color from bleed-
ing into the bear's fabric.

△ LIQUID DETERGENT dissolves completely
in cool water. Use only the foam to get rid
of surface dust and static, then wipe bear
with a washcloth rinsed in clean water.

▽ NATURAL
SPONGES can take
the place of a soft
brush or cloth.

△ A BRISTLE BRUSH is
ideal for removing loose
dust from the pile before
cleaning or washing.

◁ MACHINE WASHING is the worst
method of cleaning a jointed bear.
The fabric may be revitalized but
cardboard joints will disintegrate and
metal washers and pins will rust.
Bears that can be put safely through
the rigors of laundering are usually
unjointed and made from synthetics.

❧ GROOMING ❧
Caring for Traditional and Modern Bears

Ears are in one piece with the unjointed head.

British bear made of woven nylon plush.

Original maker's label sewn on foot-pad indicates that bear can be washed.

Unjointed arms and legs.

1960s WENDY BOSTON BEAR

Any cleaning process that involves getting fabric even slightly wet must be followed by thorough drying or the material may mold and rot. Teddies, being essentially textiles, are no exception to this rule. Dry laundered teddy bears in a mesh bag on the clothesline rather than sending the bear through a clothes dryer.

▷ A HAIR DRYER with variable settings provides an even source of gentle heat. Switch it to the coolest temperature and lowest speed. Hold it at least 12in (30cm) away from your bear, and keep it moving over the whole surface of the fabric.

△ TOWEL-DRY a long-haired bear with a thick towel to get rid of drips. Continue the drying process with an overnight sojourn in a warm place.

◁ COMB or BRUSH the pile once the fabric is completely dry. A soft-bristled brush and nylon comb are best for real mohair plush bears.

△ SYNTHETIC FABRICS on a knitted backing are quite robust and need not be handled as gently as woven plush. After drying, use a stiff natural bristle brush to restore the pile.

△ COTTON PLUSH should not be washed, but can be reconditioned using a suede brush.

◁ A SUEDE BRUSH has short, fine wire "bristles" that separate the fibers of the fabric. Brush firmly in the direction of the pile.

SOFT CLOTH ▷ polishes glass or button eyes.

◁ COTTON SWABS are handy for getting the last drops of water out of tiny crevices.

❧·BEAR WEAR·❧

Accessories for Traditional and Modern Bears

New button eyes replace original black boot buttons.

Elderly bear has been sympathetically restored.

Golden mohair plush has lost most of its pile.

Blue velvet suit, trimmed with lace, protects worn fabric.

PRE-1910 STEIFF BEAR

Every bear is enhanced by a bit of ornamentation. It can be as simple as a brightly colored ribbon bow around its neck or as grand as a designer outfit. Clothing has a practical purpose, too, as it protects the fabric from the general wear and tear that even affectionate handling will cause. It is also useful for disguising imperfections in a bear.

▷ **RIBBONS**
come in an
enormous variety of
colors, patterns,
finishes, and widths.
Use them on their own,
braided together, or as
trimmings for hand-
sewn garments.

▷ **LACE,** slotted
with ribbon,
ties into a frilly
collar.

△ **BELLS** are
jolly, strung on
pretty ribbon and
tied around
the neck.

△ **MINIATURE**
SPECTACLES and
accessories are
available from
toy suppliers.

△ **HAND-SEWN**
GARMENTS have a
personal appeal when made
from scraps of your old clothes. Or
buy a remnant of a really expensive
fabric, such as embroidered brocade
– just a small piece will make a
gorgeous jacket or vest.

▷ **STRETCHY**
SOCKS can cover
footpads that are
past repair.

❧ · STORAGE · ❧
Caring for Traditional and Modern Bears

Careful surface washing has restored the fluffiness of the pile.

Repaired, washed, and groomed bear, ready for storage.

Lace collar and ribbon bow add a nice finishing touch.

New paw and footpads made of felt.

1930S PINK MOHAIR PLUSH BEAR

eddies and hugs go naturally together, but handling an antique bear does not prolong its life. Instead, store it in a warm, dry place with a constant temperature and check its condition often. The worst place for a bear is on a bed, where it will be moved frequently. Keep bears in a dust-free environment away from direct sunlight.

▽ PLASTIC BAGS are for brief storage only. Seal a moth-eaten bear in a plastic bag with mothballs to kill insects.

△ LARVAE CASINGS, usually found in snug places, reveal the presence of beetles or moths.

◁ MOTHBALLS act rapidly to kill moths.

◁ BROWN PAPER tied with string lets the bear breathe and allows moisture to evaporate.

△ CEDAR is a natural moth repellent.

▽ WHITE TISSUE PAPER protects a fragile bear that is to be stored in a box. Use the acid-free type that does not deteriorate with age.

▽ SHOE BOXES are roomy enough for a small teddy.

❧ BEAR OWNERS ❧

Dorling Kinderseley would like to thank the following people who generously lent their injured bears for photography:

- Mrs. Baker for Goldie, page 31
- Gill Della Casa for Tessa, pages 5 (bottom) and 37
- Vicki James for Louise, pages 1 and 8
- Mary-Clare Jerram for Teddy, page 27
- Mrs. Lavery for Teddy, page 14

- Gillian Lister for Edward, page 10
- Mrs. Meeke for Max, page 12
- Mrs. Pearce for Rupert, pages 28 and 38
- Judy Sparrow for Albert, pages 4, 34, and 39; Lucy, page 36; Rowan, pages 1 and 30; and Timmy, page 20
- Mrs. Spencer for David, pages 3 and 16
- Mrs. Tuke for Wingo, pages 5 (top) and 26
- Paul and Rosemary Volpp for Sir Loved A Lot, page 6, and Inky, page 22
- Leah Ward for Billy, page 24
- Mrs. Whellams for Michael, page 41
- Lynnet Wilson for Cully, page 32

❧ USEFUL ADDRESSES ❧

The following addresses are given in good faith, but are not intended as recommendations. Before sending a bear for restoration, satisfy yourself that the repairer is capable of carrying out the work to your own satisfaction. Neither the author nor the publisher can accept responsibility for the quality of any work that is carried out.

Note: If you mail your bear (but it is safer to deliver personally), always register and insure the package; call the repairer and describe the bear's condition; confirm the repairer's address; pack the bear with all the appropriate loose parts and details of the problems.

Judy Sparrow
The Bear Museum
38 Dragon Street, Petersfield
Hampshire GU31 4JJ
England
☎ (0730) 265108

New York Doll Hospital
787 Lexington Avenue
New York, NY 10021
☎ (212) 838-7527

Franny's Teddy Bear Museum
2511 Pine Ridge Road
Naples, FL 33942
☎ (813) 598-2711

P.J. Bear's Teddy Trauma Center
Attn: Pat Johnson
2121 Contra Costa Avenue
Santa Rosa, CA 95405
☎ (707) 578-8809

By Diane
1126 Ibon Avenue
Endicott, NY 13760
☎ (607) 754-0391

MAGAZINES
The Teddy Bear and Friends
Hobby House Press
900 Frederick Street
Cumberland, MD 21502
☎ (301) 759-3770

Teddy Bear Review
Collector Communications Corp.
P.O. Box 1239
Hanover, PA 17331
☎ (717) 633-7333

❧ · INDEX · ❧

~ A, B, C ~

acrylic waste stuffing 29
artificial silk plush 14
bells 35
boot-button eyes 6
brushing 31
cardboard reinforcement 17
clipping pile 13
clockwork 23
clothing, as protection 5
cotton plush 15
cotton waste 14

~ D, E, F~

disk and pin joint 21
distressed mohair 13
dust-free environment 36
embroidered eyes 9
eye color 6
fake Rexine 17
felt pads 16
fur, real 12

~ G, H, I~

glass eyes 6
growler 25
hand-sewn clothes 35
hand-stitched nose and mouth 10
head, movable 20

~ J, K, L ~

kapok stuffing 28
lace 35
ladder stitch 27
leatherette 18
leather nose patch 10
limb seams 26
limbs, movable 20

~ M, N, O ~

main body seam 26
Masonite joint disks 21
mohair plush 12
molded nose 10
music box 23
nylon 14
nylon plush 19

~ P, R ~

patching 13
paw pads 10
pile, restoring 13
plastic-button eyes 7
plastic foam stuffing 29
plastic joints 21
plastic squeaker 25
polyester stuffing 25
polyester wadding 28
Rexine footpads 16
ribbons 35

~ S, T ~

safety eyes 8
safety noses 11
safety standards 28
shank and washer eyes 8
shanked eyes 7
sheepskin 10
sheepskin, repairing 15
sponging 31
squeaker 23
suede 12
suede brush 33
suedette 18
synthetic fabrics 15
synthetic velvet 19

tilt growler 23
tin nose 10

~ U, V, W ~

unjointed bears 20

velveteen pads 18
voice box 22
washable bears 32
wired eyes 7
wood-wool stuffing 22

❧ ACKNOWLEDGMENTS ❧

Dorling Kindersley would like to thank Judy Sparrow for supplying
most of the materials for photography.

We would also like to thank the following for their help:
Christabel Grimmer and Oakley Fabrics Ltd. for supplying materials
for photography; Andrea Fair for ferrying teddies to and from The Bear
Museum; Irene Lyford, Susan Thompson, and Ray Rogers for editorial
assistance; Pauline Bayne and Sam Grimmer for design assistance; Peter
Howlett and Alastair Wardle for their DTP expertise.

All photographs by Matthew Ward except: Jim Coit 6, 22;
Roland Kemp 7 (step-by-step), 10, 18, 21 (step-by-step), 32.

Border illustrations by Pauline Bayne.
Illustrated letters by Gillie Newman.